Low Carb Dessert Cookbook

Delicious Low Carb Dessert Recipes To Help You Burn Fat

Table of Contents

Orange Cookies

Coconut Cookies

Almond Flour Blueberry Muffins

Vanilla Meringue Cookies

Cream Cheese Sugar Cookies

Low Carb Ginger Snaps

Introduction

The low carb diet is one of the most proven and effective diets for losing weight, yet some people find this diet difficult to stay on because of the assumption that this diet means giving up tasty and delicious dessert recipes. This is not true however, there are plenty of tasty low carb dessert recipes out there that taste just as good as there non-low carb counter parts.

You can still enjoy mouthwatering cheesecakes and delicious chocolate chip cookies while being on the low carb diet. This low carb cookbook is filled with these tasty dessert recipes, and will make you forget that you are even on the low carb diet!

We hope you enjoy these delicious low carb recipes, and good luck!

Chapter 1 - Low Carb Pie And Cake Recipes

No Bake Cheesecake

Ingredients

1 packet unflavored gelatin

3/4 cup vanilla flavored sugar free syrup

24 ounces cream cheese, softened

1 cup heavy cream, whipped

Graham cracker pie crust (see recipe below)

Directions

Prepare the crust according to the recipe for a baked crust. In a small pot, sprinkle the gelatin over 1/2 cup syrup and let soften 5 minutes.

Heat and stir over low heat to dissolve the gelatin completely. Beat the cream cheese with the remaining 1/4 cup syrup until creamy.

Gradually beat in the gelatin mixture. Chill until slightly thickened, about 1 hour, gently whisking occasionally to prevent lumps.

Fold in the whipped cream.

Pour into the crust and chill until set for approximately 2 hours.

Nutrition: 368 Calories; 37g Fat; 7g Protein; 4g Carbohydrate; per 1/12 of recipe

Low Carb Graham Cracker Crust

Ingredients

3 oz almond flour, 3/4 cup

3 tbsp flax meal

1/4 tsp salt

6 tbsp butter, melted

1/3 cup granular Splenda or equivalent liquid Splenda

Directions

Mix the dry ingredients in a small bowl. Add the liquid Splenda, if using, to the melted butter; pour over the dry ingredients.

Mix well and spread in a 9" pie plate or springform pan. Bake at 375° about 10-12 minutes until set and lightly browned.

Cool, then fill the pie.

For baked pies, chill unbaked crust 1 hour before filling and baking.

Nutrition: 153 Calories; 15g Fat; 3g Protein; 4g Carbohydrate; per 1/8 of recipe

Low Carb Cream Cheese Pound Cake

Ingredients

1/2 cup butter, softened

4 oz cream cheese, softened

1 cup granular Splenda or equivalent liquid Splenda

5 eggs, room temperature

1 tsp lemon extract

1 tsp vanilla

6 1/2 oz almond flour, 1 1/2 cups plus 2 tablespoons

1 teaspoon baking powder

Dash of salt

Directions

Cream the butter, cream cheese and Splenda with an electric mixer. Add the eggs, one at a time; blend in the extracts.

Mix the almond flour, salt and baking powder; add to the egg mixture a little at a time. Pour into a well greased 9-inch round cake pan, spring form pan, or bundt pan.

Bake at 350F° 50-55 minutes. The cake will be golden brown and firm to the touch when done.

Nutrition: 331 Calories; 30g Fat; 10g Protein; 4.4g Carbohydrate; per 1/8 of recipe

Low Carb Pumpkin Pie

Ingredients

15 oz can pumpkin

2 eggs

1/2 cup granular Splenda or equivalent liquid Splenda

1/4 cup caramel or vanilla sugar free syrup

1/2 cup heavy cream

1/4 cup water or 1/4 cup heavy cream

1/4-1/2 tsp salt

1 tsp cinnamon

1/2 tsp ginger

1/4 tsp cloves

Directions

Mix all of the ingredients in a medium bowl; beat well with an electric mixer. Pour into a buttered 9-inch pie plate.

Bake at 350F° 45-55 minutes, until a knife inserted in the center comes out clean. Cool on a rack, then chill well before serving.

Serve with whipped cream, if desired.

Nutrition: 114 Calories; 10g Fat; 3g Protein; 5g Carbohydrate; per 1/8 of recipe

No Bake Blueberry Cheesecake

Ingredients

1 - 8 oz package cream cheese

8 oz whipping cream

3/4 cup blueberries

1/2 cup splenda

Directions

In a bowl whip whipping cream until peaks form. Add Splenda. Blend in cream cheese whip until smooth.

With a spoon gently add frozen blueberries. Spoon into dessert cups.

Nutrition: 208 Calories; 21g Fat; 3g Protein; 3.3g Carbohydrate; per 1/8 of recipe

Low Carb Brownie Pie

Ingredients

4 eggs

4 tablespoons butter

4 ounces sugar free chocolate chips

1/2 teaspoon blackstrap molasses, optional *

1/2 cup Carbquik

3/4 cup granular Splenda or equivalent liquid Splenda

1 teaspoon vanilla

1/2 cup walnuts, chopped

Directions

In a small microwaveable bowl, melt the butter and chocolate about 2-4 minutes on 50% power, stirring after each minute.

Cool to room temperature. Beat the eggs, butter and chocolate with an electric mixer in a medium bowl about 30 seconds or until smooth.

Add the molasses, Carbquik, Splenda and vanilla. Beat 2 minutes. Pour into a greased 9" glass pie plate. Sprinkle with the nuts.

Bake at 350F° for 20-35 minutes or until a knife inserted in the center comes out clean.

Check the pie after 20 minutes careful not to over bake.

Cool completely, about 1 hour. Serve with whipped cream, if desired.

Nutrition: 240 Calories; 19g Fat; 8g Protein; 6g Carbohydrate; per 1/6 of recipe

New York Cheese Cake

Ingredients

32 ounces (907 grams) cream cheese, room temperature

1 cup artificial sweetener

5 large eggs, room temperature

1/3 cup (80 ml) Organic heavy whipping cream (double cream)

1 tbsp lemon zest

1 tsp pure vanilla extract

Directions

Grease, or spray with Pam, a 9 inch (23 cm) springform pan. Place the springform pan on a larger baking pan to catch any leakage while the cheesecake is baking.

Preheat oven to 350 degrees F (177 degrees C) with rack in center of oven.

For Filling: In bowl of your electric mixer place the cream cheese and sugar. Beat on medium speed until smooth (about 2 minutes), scraping down the bowl as needed.

Add the eggs, one at a time, beating well (about 30 seconds) after each addition. Scrape down the sides of the bowl. Add the whipping cream, lemon zest, vanilla extract and beat until incorporated.

Pour the filling in the greased pan. Place the cheesecake pan on a larger baking pan and place in the oven.

Bake for 15 minutes and then lower the oven temperature to 250 degrees F (120 degrees C) and continue to bake for about another 60 minutes or until firm and only the center of the cheesecake looks a little wet and jello like.

Remove from oven and carefully run a knife or spatula around the inside edge of pan to loosen the cheesecake.

Let cool completely before covering with plastic wrap. Refrigerate several hours.

Nutrition: 354 Calories; 31g Fat; 8g Protein; 3.4g Carbohydrate; per 1/12 of recipe

Low Carb Pumpkin Cheesecake

Ingredients

16 oz cream cheese

6 eggs

1/2 cup sugar free maple syrup

1 cup canned unsweetened pumpkin

3/8 tsp Stevia extract powder

1 tsp cinnamon

1/4 tsp nutmeg

Directions

Preheat oven to 350F. Combine all ingredients in a mixer and blend until smooth.

Pour into a deep dish pie pan that has been sprayed with non stick cooking spray. Bake for 50 - 55 minutes or until center is set.

Remove from oven. let cool then chill completely.

Nutrition: 267 Calories; 24g Fat; 9g Protein; 5.7g Carbohydrate; per 1/8 of recipe

Almond Spice Cake

Ingredients

1 cup milk

1 tbsp. white vinegar

2 tbsp. butter – softened

2 tbsp shortening – softened

3/4 cup Splenda granulated

1/2 tsp vanilla

1 large egg

1/2 tsp ground cinnamon

1/8 tsp ground cloves

1/8 tsp ground ginger

1/8 tsp ground allspice

1/2 tsp baking powder

1/2 tsp baking soda

1 cup almond flour

Directions

Preheat oven to 350 degrees. Prepare 8" square baking dish by either spraying with Baker's Joy or grease the sides.

Mix vineger and milk. Set aside.

In medium mixing bowl, cream together butter and shortening. Blend in Splenda. Add vanilla and egg. Mix until well blended.

Add spices, baking powder, and baking soda. Stir to mix. Begin adding almond flour and milk mixture alternately, stirring until just mixed after each addition.

Pour into baking dish. Bake for 40 minutes at 350 degrees. Allow to cool on a wire rack for 1 hour. Cake will be extremely moist and very dense.

Nutrition: 143 Calories; 12g Fat; 4g Protein; 5.2g Carbohydrate; per 1/9 of recipe

Keylime Pie

Ingredients

1 small package sugar free lime jello

1/2 cup boiling water

8 oz cream cheese, softened

1 tbsp lime juice, one small lime

Lime peel, finely grated, one small lime

1/2 cup heavy cream

Directions

Dissolve the jello in the boiling water, stirring for 3 minutes. Beat the cream cheese in a medium bowl with an electric mixer until smooth.

Gradually beat the jello into the cream. Add the lime juice and rind.

Add cream and whip until fluffy. Pour into a pie plate that has been sprayed with nonstick spray. Chill until set.

Nutrition: 208 Calories; 21g Fat; 4g Protein; 3g Carbohydrate; per 1/6 of recipe

Low Carb Blueberry Coffee Cake

Ingredients

1/4 cup butter, softened

10 tsp stevia

1 egg

1 cup almond flour

1 teaspoon baking powder

1/4 tsp salt

1/2 cup milk

1 cup fresh or frozen blueberries

1 package (3 ounces) cream cheese, cubed

Directions

For batter, in a large bowl, cream butter and sugar until light and fluffy. Beat in egg.

Combine flour, baking powder and salt; gradually add to creamed mixture alternately with milk.

Stir blueberries and cream cheese into creamed mixture - batter will be thick. Transfer to a greased 8-in. square baking dish.

Bake at 375F° for 40-45 minutes or until a toothpick inserted near the center comes out clean.

Cool on a wire rack.

Nutrition: 202 Calories; 17g Fat; 5.6g Protein; 6.2g Carbohydrate; per 1/8 of recipe

Low Carb Chocolate Cake

Ingredients

Dry Ingredients
2 cups ground flax seed

1 cup Splenda

4 tsp baking powder

1/2 tsp salt

1/2 cup cocoa powder

1/2 cup almonds, ground

1/2 cup pumpkin seeds, ground

Wet Ingredients:
6 eggs, beaten

1 cup canola oil

1 cup half and half cream

1/2 cup Sour Cream

1 tbsp vanilla extract

Directions
Preheat oven to 350F

Prepare a 9x14 cake pan by lining it with parchment, or spray with nonstick cooking spray

Combine dry ingredients in a medium sized bowl. Set aside

Combine wet ingredients in blender or bowl. Add wet ingredients to dry all at once and stir together gently until a smooth batter.

Let stand about 5 minutes and then add to prepared pan.

Bake in oven 30 minutes or until toothpick inserted, comes out clean.

Makes 24 servings

Nutrition: 185 Calories; 17g Fat; 5g Protein; 6 g Carbohydrate; per 1/24 of recipe

Chapter 2 – Low Carb Cookie And Muffin Recipes

Hazelnut Cookies

Makes 15 cookies

Ingredients

2 large eggs

2/3 cup butter

1 teaspoon vanilla extract

3 tablespoons sugar substitute

1/2 cup hazelnut butter

1 teaspoon baking powder

1 pinch salt

1/3 cup sugar free dark chocolate chips

Directions

Preheat oven to 375F.

Separate the whites from the yolks and beat the whites stiff. In the bowl with the yolks add the vanilla extract and butter.

Add the sweetener and mix again.

Add Peanut butter and mix till well combined.

Add the baking powder and the salt. Then you add the chocolate chunks.

When your batter is done, gently fold in the egg whites.

Divide the dough evenly into about 15 small pieces of dough and place them on a cookie sheet.

Leave enough space for cookies to spread.

Bake for about 15 minutes at 375F.

Total Carbs: 2g per cookie

Easy Low Carb Peanut Butter Cookies

Makes 16 cookies

Ingredients

1 cup no sugar added peanut butter

1 cup sugar substitute

1 egg

1 teaspoon vanilla

Directions

Preheat oven to 350F.

Mix ingredients in a small bowl.

Drop by rounded teaspoons onto cookie sheet.

Bake at 350 degrees F for 12 minutes or until set.

Total Carbs: 4.5g per cookie

Sugar Cookies

Makes 40 cookies

Ingredients

2 ounces cream cheese

2 egg yolks

1 tablespoon butter, softened

1 teaspoon vanilla

6 (1 g) packets Splenda sugar substitute

2 tablespoons all-purpose flour

2 tablespoons wheat gluten flour (vital wheat gluten)

½ teaspoon baking powder

¾ cup almond meal, from blanched almonds

Directions

Preheat oven to 325F.

In a mixer with paddle attachment, cream together the first three ingredients until creamy and fluffy.

In a small bowl, mix together the flour, wheat gluten and baking powder. Add a pinch of salt if you like.

Once the mixture is creamed, add vanilla and mix well. Now add Splenda and mix well.

Stir in the flour mixture by hand. Lastly stir in the almond flour.

Refrigerate the dough for about 30 min to make it easier to work with.

Preheat oven to 325°F Line baking sheet with parchment.

Form small marble size balls of the dough.

Put a ball of dough on the parchment and using the flat bottom of a glass press to flatten. Using a piece of parchment between the glass and dough will prevent it from sticking.

Bake in the oven for 8-10 minutes until the edges for golden.

Total carbs: 1g per cookie

Quick Chocolate Cookies

Makes 18 cookies

Ingredients

1 ⅓ cups whey chocolate protein powder

3 tablespoons soy flour

¼ cup butter

4 ounces cream cheese

¾ cup vanilla-flavored skim milk or soymilk

1 teaspoon baking powder

3 tablespoons Splenda sugar substitute

½ cup walnuts

Directions

Preheat oven to 325F.

Melt butter and cream cheese in microwave Add Splenda and stir until smooth

Mix in remaining ingredients, add nuts.

Bake at 325F for 10 minutes.

Total Carbs: 3g per cookie

Cranberry Muffins

Ingredients

1 cup whole fresh cranberries

1.25 cup flax seed meal

1 tsp baking powder

3 tbsp cinnamon

1 tsp nutmeg

1/2 tsp salt

1/2 cup splenda

4 large eggs

1/4 cup olive oil

1/2 cup Vanilla sugar free syrup

1 tbsp vanilla

Directions

Pre heat oven to 350F.

Liberally butter the muffin tins, makes 12 muffins with enough batter to make 3 more if you want to dirty up an extra muffin tin Do not use muffin liners they will stick.

Pour boiling water over cranberries and let sit for 5 minutes. Mix wet ingredients and dry ingredients separately and then combine, except the cranberries, let mixture stand for about 10 minutes to thicken. Fold in cranberries once thickened a little bit.

Fill each muffin cup up about 1/2 to 3/4 full.

Bake for about 17 minutes or until toothpick comes out clean.

Total Carbs: 6g per muffin

Orange Cookies

Makes 36 cookies

Ingredients

3/4 cup Swerve

3/4 cup butter softened

3 eggs

1/2 cup coconut flour

1 1/2 teaspoons baking powder

1/4 teaspoon baking soda

1/4 cup unsweetened dried cranberries

1/2 cup macadamia nuts chopped

1 1/2 tsp dried grated orange zest

Directions

In large mixing bowl, beat together sweetener, butter, and eggs until well combined.

Add coconut flour, baking powder, and baking soda. Beat on low or with spoon until well blended.

Stir in cranberries, nuts, and orange zest. Shape into round mounds with cookie scoop or hands.

Place at least one inch apart on parchment or silicone lined cookie sheet. Press each mound down slightly with fingers or bottom of glass to flatten.

Bake at 350°F for 8-10 minutes or until edges have started to brown. Cool for a few minutes, then transfer to cooling rack. Will keep for a week in the refrigerator.

Total carbs: 2g

Coconut Cookies

Makes 20 cookies

Ingredients

1 ounce almond flour

2 ounces unsweetened coconut, ground fine

1/8 teaspoon salt

2 tablespoons granular Splenda

1/8 teaspoon vanilla

1 egg white

Directions

Mix all of the ingredients well in a small bowl. Everything should be moist and the dough should hold together.

Drop the dough by teaspoons onto a parchment or silicone lined 12x17" baking sheet. Roll each piece of dough into a ball.

Cover the balls with plastic wrap and take a baking powder can, that has about an 1/8" rim around the bottom, and press down firmly over each ball of dough.

Be sure to press all the way down to the baking sheet. Peel off the plastic wrap and repeat until all the crackers have been shaped.

Bake at 325° for 15-20 minutes, or until golden brown.

Total carbs: 2g

Almond Flour Blueberry Muffins

Ingredients

2 cups almond flour

2 tsp baking powder

¼ tsp salt

½ cup butter, unsalted

4 large eggs

1/3 cup splenda,

1 cup blueberries

1/3 cup water

Directions

Preheat oven to 350F.

Grease a muffin pan. Mix all dry ingredients well. Mix all wet ingredients well. Add the wet ingredients to the dry.

Add the blueberries last. Fill muffin tins 2/3 full.

Bake for 20 minutes.

Total carbs: 4g per muffin

Vanilla Meringue Cookies

Makes 20 cookies

Ingredients
4 egg whites

2 teaspoons vanilla

1/4 teaspoon salt

18 teaspoons Truvia

Directions
Put the egg whites, vanilla and salt in a large metal bowl. Beat with an electric mixer on MEDIUM speed until foamy.

Gradually beat in the Truvia. Increase the speed to HIGH and beat until the mixture is very thick for about 10 minutes.

Drop the meringue mixture by large spoonfuls on a large parchment paper lined baking sheet.

Bake at 300F for 30 minutes or until they are crisp.

Total carbs: 2g

Cream Cheese Sugar Cookies

Makes 75 cookies

Ingredients

1 cup butter

3/4 cup sugar substitute

4 ounces cream cheese softened

1 egg

2 cups almond flour

1/2 cup coconut flour

1 teaspoon vanilla extract

Directions

Cream the butter and sweetener until light and fluffy.

Beat in the cream cheese. Add in the egg.

Stir in the the flours, then mix in the vanilla. Chill dough for at least 4 hours .

Squeeze dough out of cookie press or roll out into a cookie log and slice.

Bake at 350F until cookies begin to brown

Total Carbs: 4g per cookies

Low Carb Ginger Snaps

Makes 42 cookies

Ingredients
1 1/2 cups almond flour

3/4 cup coconut flour

2 teaspoons baking powder

3/4 teaspoon ground cinnamon

1/2 teaspoon ground cloves

1/4 teaspoon salt

3/4 cup butter softened

3/4 cup Sukrin Gold

1 egg

Directions
In large bowl, combine almond flour, coconut flour, baking powder, cinnamon, cloves, and salt.

In another large mixing bowl, cream together butter and Sukrin Gold.

Beat egg into butter mixture.

Slowly add dry mixture into butter mixture. Knead into a dough.

Scoop into balls and roll in Sukrin.

Place dough balls or scoops onto parchment paper lined cookie sheet or use non-stick silicon baking sheet leaving with adequate spacing.

Press each ball down with flat bottom glass. Bake at 350 F for about 8 to 10 minutes.

Total carbs: 2g per cookie